SERIES 228

In this book, we uncover the remarkable
history of the ancient Romans, from
dramatic gladiator fights and chariot races
to huge armies and amazing architecture.

LADYBIRD BOOKS

UK | USA | Canada | Ireland | Australia
India | New Zealand | South Africa
Ladybird Books is part of the Penguin Random House group of companies
whose addresses can be found at global.penguinrandomhouse.com.
www.penguin.co.uk   www.puffin.co.uk   www.ladybird.co.uk

Penguin
Random House
UK

First published 2022
001
Copyright © Ladybird Books Ltd, 2022
Printed in China

The authorized representative in the EEA is Penguin Random House Ireland,
Morrison Chambers, 32 Nassau Street, Dublin D02 YH68

A CIP catalogue record for this book is available from the British Library
ISBN: 978-0-241-54418-1
All correspondence to:
Ladybird Books
Penguin Random House Children's
One Embassy Gardens, 8 Viaduct Gardens
London SW11 7BW

The **Romans**

A Ladybird Book

Written by Samia Gundkalli
with historical consultant, Dr April Pudsey

Illustrated by Beatrice Cerocchi

The founding of Rome

Have you ever wondered where the English alphabet that we use today came from, or how we can tell which month of the year it is? We owe these things — as well as many other parts of our everyday lives — to the Romans.

The Romans were a group of people who lived over 2,000 years ago. Their name comes from the place where they first lived: the city of Rome, found in the region now known as Italy. There are many legends about how this city came into being, but the most famous is the myth of Romulus and Remus. Romulus and Remus were the twin sons of the Roman god of war, Mars. Fearful that the children would overthrow him, the king ordered for the twins to be abandoned in a basket on the River Tiber, but the brothers somehow survived. After being cared for by a she-wolf, Romulus and Remus were adopted and raised by a shepherd.

Many years later, Romulus and Remus returned to the place where they had been rescued as children and decided to create their own city. However, the brothers argued over exactly where to build it. Desperate for victory, Romulus killed Remus, and in 753 BCE declared his own new city, which he named "Rome" after himself.

Today, we understand myths to be imaginary stories, but the tale of Romulus and Remus was extremely special to Romans, and it formed an important part of their identity.

Early Rome

Unlike the dramatic events in the myth of Romulus and Remus, it is likely that Rome was founded much more slowly and gradually. Most historians think that small tribes began to build clusters of huts surrounding the River Tiber in central Italy, which eventually formed villages. As these villages spread across the hills, the city of Rome began to take shape. We know that Romulus was its first king during the eighth century BCE.

Although the Tiber often flooded, its banks were still an ideal place for the city to develop and grow. The river provided a valuable supply of fresh water, which people could use as drinking water and for farming. Above all, the Tiber was important for trade as it allowed ships to carry goods to the coast and across the Mediterranean Sea, to and from places such as North Africa. Years later, a city called Ostia became Rome's main seaport. Its location at the mouth of the river was perfect for trading, as well as for defence against Rome's enemies.

The Romans were also lucky to have some very influential neighbours, such as the Greeks and Egyptians. These civilizations already had successful societies and trading systems, which the Romans could cleverly take inspiration from and engage with.

The Roman Republic

Seven different kings ruled over Rome following Romulus's death, but not all of them were popular. Following a rebellion in 509 BCE to overthrow the king, Lucius Tarquinius Superbus, a new, more organized type of government was put into place. It was called the "Roman Republic".

In the republic, certain people could vote to choose who they wanted in power, and there were more laws that citizens had to follow. The Law of the Twelve Tables was introduced around 450 BCE and is thought to be one of the earliest sets of laws written down. It included rules on people's rights, property and religion.

Two men called "consuls" were elected to hold the most power in the republic and had ultimate control of the city. They followed the advice of a group of wealthy, older men called the "senate", who met regularly to debate new laws.

The republic had set out to give more of a say to its citizens, but in reality the system was not equal. Your level of power depended on your gender and how much money you had. Common people, known as "plebeians", could not elect their own leaders or act as consuls for many years. Women and enslaved people could not vote at all. Hortensia, the daughter of a well-known consul, was one of the only women to have played a role in politics when she gave a speech challenging the taxes placed on women in 42 BCE.

The Roman army

The Romans had big ambitions to conquer new lands. They needed a strong army to achieve this, and modern-day historians believe Rome had one of the most forceful armies in history.

The Roman army was extremely organized and well trained, and, at its largest, it is believed to have had over 450,000 people. The army was formed of units called "legions", with each legion being made up of around 5,000 soldiers. A soldier could either be a legionary or an auxiliary. Legionaries were Roman citizens and formed the highest rank of recruits, while auxiliaries were non-Roman citizens and typically came from countries outside of Italy, many of which later became part of the Roman Empire. Once an auxiliary had served in the army for 20 to 25 years, they would receive an award called a "military diploma" and officially become a Roman citizen. The army quickly formed a large part of everyday life and even toys that soldiers' children played with – such as wooden horses – were styled on the military world.

Each piece of a soldier's equipment was specially adapted for battle. The armour was made from strong iron that was excellent at protecting the soldiers' bodies, while their sharp javelins could be thrown towards enemies from long distances. A legionary's entire armour and weaponry could have weighed up to a massive 45 kilograms (7 st, 1 lb)!

Helmet

Armour

Javelin

Shield

Sword

Tunic

Julius Caesar

As the Roman army proved its strength, many of its generals began to fight for greater power, especially in politics. One of the most famous was a man called Julius Caesar.

Caesar was an impressive army commander who had conquered a region called Gaul. In 49 BCE, the senate ordered Caesar to return to Rome without his army. On the journey, Caesar reached the Rubicon river in north Italy, which was the border between Rome and Gaul, and made a life-changing decision. He went against orders and crossed the river with his army right behind him, sparking a civil war in Rome.

In ancient Rome, dictators had been appointed during emergencies and were given total control over the city. Once Caesar had arrived in Rome, he made himself dictator. He went on to make several changes to the government and did more to help poorer people in society. He also issued special coins, which many leaders often did to demonstrate their ambition to others. Caesar was also responsible for introducing the calendar that inspired the one we still use today. In fact, the English names for the twelve months all come from Latin, the ancient Roman language, and the month of July is derived from Julius Caesar's name. Yet Caesar had made many enemies as dictator. His rule came to an end in 44 BCE when he was killed by a group of ambitious politicians thought to be jealous of his power.

A roman coin, known as a silver denarius, showing the
Roman god Saturn on one side and an eagle on the other.
These images showed that Caesar's army was strong.

The end of the republic

Julius Caesar's death sparked another bitter civil war in Rome. Octavian, who was Caesar's great-nephew, wanted to remove those who had murdered his uncle from power, and establish rule for himself instead. He joined forces with Mark Antony, a Roman general and politician, and Lepidus, a statesman, to defeat Caesar's killers and end the war.

At first, the three men decided to share their new-found power, but Octavian soon accused Lepidus of trying to form a rebellion against him and sent him into exile. Octavian had been in charge of looking after the western part of the republic and Mark Antony in charge of the eastern part, but their relationship quickly turned sour, too. Mark Antony was accused of conspiring with the Egyptian queen, Cleopatra, and the Roman senate eventually declared a war against Egypt in 32 BCE. The following year, Octavian defeated Mark Antony and the Egyptians during a tense sea battle fought at Actium, just off the coast of Greece. Octavian presented the Battle of Actium as his final triumph over Egypt, and issued coins to display this victory to the Roman people.

With this success, Octavian's path to power now lay clear. In 27 BCE, the senate gave Octavian the title of "imperator" – meaning "emperor" – and a new name of Augustus. Augustus had become the first emperor of Rome, and the Roman Republic officially came to an end.

The Roman Empire

The emperor ruled an empire, which was a group of many countries. During his forty-year rule, Emperor Augustus helped transform Rome into the grand centre of his new empire. He built new public buildings, theatres and temples, ordered the creation of a postal system and set up teams of firefighters and guards to keep crime at bay. He also ordered new roads to be built to replace the city's narrow streets. Roman roads were famously flat, straight and well built, which also meant that soldiers, merchants and traders could move around the empire more easily. A new system of taxes was introduced, as well as clearer laws around marriage and religion. Although many people still lived difficult lives of poverty, for many others, daily Roman life had begun to change like never before.

Emperors were responsible for making sure their empire was seen as the most powerful, and as time passed, more land was conquered. Under Augustus's rule, the empire took control of areas in Europe, Egypt and parts of what is now the Middle East. This meant that trading with other countries was easier and made the empire richer, especially for the wealthy, elite ruling classes.

The Roman Empire was at its largest around 117 CE. It is thought to have spanned around 2 million square miles (5 million km^2), and over sixty million people lived under its rule – huge numbers of whom were enslaved by the Romans.

The conquest of Britain

The Romans had wanted to conquer Britain for many years, in search of resources such as wool, silver and gold. Despite two unsuccessful attempts during Caesar's rule, Emperor Claudius decided to invade Britain once more. In 43 CE, the mighty Roman army arrived in Kent and marched to Colchester, where they finally defeated the Celtic tribe that ruled Britain.

In the four-hundred years that followed, the Romans established their rule in Britain. They built new roads, shared laws and declared *Londinium* – the city we know today as London – to be the capital of their new territory. Hadrian's Wall was also built by Emperor Hadrian to protect Roman Britain from unconquered territories to the north. The ruins of the wall, which was 73 miles (117 km) long, can still be seen today. An inscription was also found near a fort at Burgh by Sands on Hadrian's Wall, known as *Aballava* to the Romans, describing an African soldier who had been stationed there. This shows that people from across the empire were part of the Roman army in Britain at this time.

Boudicca, the queen of the Iceni tribe in eastern England, famously led a major revolt against the Romans around 60 CE. Furious that the Romans had taken her entire kingdom for themselves after her husband's death, Boudicca decided to fight back. Her tribe was eventually defeated, but the rebellion had posed a massive threat to Roman forces.

Pompeii

Pompeii was a lively, bustling town to the south of Rome. It stood at the foot of a giant volcano called Mount Vesuvius, which had been dormant for many years. But on the fateful morning of 24 August 79 CE, Vesuvius suddenly erupted. Pompeii and its neighbouring towns, such as Herculaneum, were covered in tons of lava, stones and hot rock. Ash and debris then rained down for almost two days, burying everything in sight. While many people managed to escape, it is believed that more than 2,000 Pompeians lost their lives in the violent eruption. Pompeii was never rebuilt, and the ash-covered town lay untouched for almost 1,700 years.

It was only in the late sixteenth century that archaeologists began to uncover the ruins at Pompeii. To their surprise, they found that the ash had preserved much of the town. They found houses, shops, baths and theatres, and everyday items such as mirrors, coins and pens. The remains of loaves of bread were even found in a preserved bakery! Many of the taverns and other buildings had paintings on their walls, which showed women serving drinks and men playing dice games. Some walls even had graffiti written on them describing local politics and gladiator games. Because of these discoveries, we know much more about how people lived during Roman times, and Pompeii is now a popular destination for tourists from around the world.

Entertainment at the Colosseum

The Romans enjoyed many different kinds of entertainment, and performances of all sorts drew in big audiences. Shows were often held in open-air arenas called "amphitheatres". The largest amphitheatre in the Roman Empire was called the Colosseum. It took almost ten years to build and once completed, the Colosseum could welcome up to 50,000 spectators. The Colosseum sometimes hosted musicians, and beast hunters who battled wild animals, but gladiator fights were its most popular attraction.

Gladiators were professional, specially trained fighters who were often forced to fight in front of an audience. There were many different ranks of gladiators, each with their own set of weapons and clothing. Most gladiators were either criminals or enslaved people who were there against their will, but some had volunteered to fight. Evidence from 100 to 200 CE also shows that women sometimes fought as gladiators, too. A female gladiator was called a "gladiatrix".

When a fighter became seriously injured, they could look to the crowd for mercy. We can't be sure what signals were made, but many historians think that the crowd would wave their handkerchiefs if they wanted the gladiator to live but turned their thumbs down if they wanted them to be killed. If the emperor was in the audience, the final decision lay in his hands. Since they were expensive to train, many gladiators were allowed to live.

Chariot racing

Chariot racing was another hugely popular competition enjoyed by the Romans. Originally invented by the Greeks, this sport was fast-paced and dangerous, adding to the thrill for the crowd.

Chariot races in Rome were held at the Circus Maximus, which could host up to 250,000 people – one of the largest sports arenas ever built. There were several tiers of seating inside the Circus, with the emperor and most important senators watching the race from special boxes and the highest seats. In the middle of the oval-shaped racetrack was the *spina* – a barrier for the chariots to race around.

Competitors drove the chariots, which were small, two-wheeled vehicles that would usually be drawn by four horses. During the early days of the Roman Empire, chariots raced in teams that were organized into four different colours: white, blue, red and green. People would often have one particular team that they always supported, just like many of us have our favourite sports teams! Up to twelve chariots would compete per race, and they would have to be the first to complete seven laps around the Circus to win. A charioteer named Gaius Appuleius Diocles, who won over 1,400 races during his career, is thought to be one of the most well-paid athletes of all time.

A trip to the theatre

During the early days of the republic, plays were usually only held on special occasions and took place in a town square called the "forum". However, in the age of the empire, plays became more popular and began to be performed more regularly. Theatres that could host larger plays and bigger audiences began to be constructed from 55 CE. In these new buildings, the audience would sit on seats in a semi-circle that faced a stage in the centre called the *pulpitum*, similar to the way audiences are seated in modern-day theatres. It was designed this way so that more people in the audience could hear the play.

Just like many other parts of its society, Roman theatre was also heavily influenced by the Greeks. There were several types of play performed in Rome, but the most popular were pantomimes, comedies and tragedies. A North African playwright called Terence, who had come to Rome after being enslaved, was well known for his comedies. Another playwright called Plautus wrote several famous comedies as well, while a man called Seneca was best known for tragedy. Both Terence and Seneca are thought to have influenced some of the works of the famous English playwright, William Shakespeare.

The stories that are told through Roman plays reveal a lot about their way of life, which is why people continue to study and perform them.

Home life

Leisure and entertainment were valued by all Romans, but it is important to remember that not everyone enjoyed the same kind of lifestyle and privileges. Poorer Romans in cities lived in crowded flats called *insulae*, which were often cramped and dirty. Many also lived in villages and the countryside, where they earned money through farming and selling crops.

A typical wealthy family in Rome would live in a house known as a *domus*. A *domus* was usually large and lavish, and featured multiple rooms, each with its own purpose. A grand entrance led to the *atrium*, which was an open courtyard typically used for welcoming guests. Leading off from the *atrium* were multiple bedrooms and a study.

Enslaved people – who were usually captured during a war – worked for rich Romans and were considered to be the property of those that enslaved them. They could only be freed if their enslavers allowed it, but some enslaved people who had received an education could earn their own money to eventually buy their own freedom.

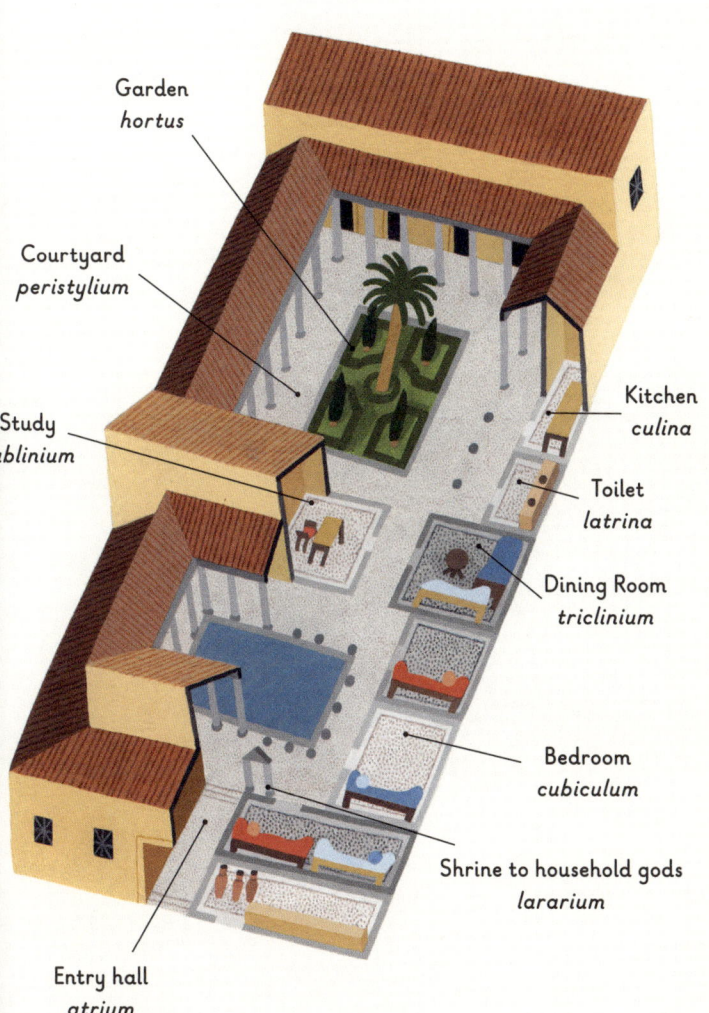

Garden
hortus

Courtyard
peristylium

Study
ablinium

Kitchen
culina

Toilet
latrina

Dining Room
triclinium

Bedroom
cubiculum

Shrine to household gods
lararium

Entry hall
atrium

Banquets

The Romans loved to socialize with one another after the working day was finished, especially over food and drink. Wealthy members of Roman society regularly held decadent evening feasts called "banquets", which gave their hosts the perfect place to show how influential and important they were.

The meal was typically set out on a dining table surrounded by low couches, where guests would lie down and eat the food with their hands. As banquets were very special occasions, men would wear special dresses called "togas" over their tunics, while women wore a traditional dress called a *palla*.

There were usually three courses: a starter, a main and a dessert, with a variety of different foods on offer. Exotic animals such as pheasants, lobsters, peacocks and flamingos would be served, often eaten with a special fish sauce called *garum*. Desserts would include cakes, fruits and nuts.

Hosts would also arrange entertainment to impress their guests, such as music performances, dances and poetry recitals. A great party could sometimes last for up to ten hours!

Learning

Schools were set up during the Roman Republic, but as families had to pay for their children to attend, only the children of the very wealthy received an education.

From the ages of seven to eleven, students learned how to read, write and count at the primary school, or *ludus*. Class usually started early in the morning and finished around midday. Roman children also had to attend school seven days a week! Notes were taken on a wax tablet with a *stylus* – a special type of pen – and lessons were taught in Latin. Many of the words we use across the world today come from this ancient language; for example, the word "school" comes from the Latin word *schola*. Some boys continued their studies with a teacher called a *grammaticus*, studying subjects such as history and athletics to prepare for careers in the army or politics. Elsewhere in the Roman Empire, schools focused on other subjects. In Egypt, some wealthy parents sent their children to a famous school that had existed under the Ancient Greeks. Here, children were taught how to read and write Greek, as well as art and literature.

Roman boys and girls were expected to achieve different things in their lives, so were not offered equal opportunities. While some girls could attend primary school, their studies usually finished when they left, and they would be taught skills at home instead. Around the empire, children were also taught trades like weaving and hair-cutting.

Medicine

The Romans made important discoveries in science and medicine, such as learning how to prevent illness and improving public hygiene. A Greek man named Claudius Galen moved to Rome in 162 CE, where he eventually became the personal doctor for the emperor. Galen thought that by dissecting animals and finding out more about their organs and bones, he could find out more about humans, too. He is now known for making significant medical discoveries – such as learning that arteries carry blood around our bodies – and his findings paved the way for future doctors and scientists to learn more about the human body.

Hospitals were also built in the empire to treat soldiers who had been hurt in battle. Roman surgeons would use vinegar to clean soldiers' wounds and developed medical tools to practise procedures. Some women also worked as midwives.

Many Greeks believed that if they worshipped the god of medicine, Asclepius, their sicknesses would be cured. These beliefs were eventually adopted within the Roman Empire, too, with many believing in the healing powers of this god. Romans believed different plants and herbs could cure their illnesses. For example, garlic was supposed to keep the heart healthy, marsh mallow was used to settle coughs and chamomile was thought to ease headaches.
Do you recognize any of the plants and herbs on the opposite page? How might we use them today?

Marsh mallow

Rosemary

Chamomile

Blackberry

Garlic

Roman baths

The Romans were one of the first civilizations to create a fresh water supply that its citizens could use for drinking and bathing. The water was brought to the city by a system of pipes called "aqueducts". Aqueducts carried water from a river or spring to a large storage tank, which connected to a set of pipes that would then carry the water to fountains or baths. The first aqueduct was built in Rome in 312 BCE, and by 3 CE there were eleven aqueducts across the entire city.

Most towns had a public bath for Romans to visit. The baths were not just a place to get clean, but also a hub for socializing, relaxing and doing business. Inside, you would find large swimming pools, steam rooms and saunas. This practice has actually inspired our modern-day spas!

During a typical trip, most people would first relax in a warm room called the *tepidarium*, followed by a visit to a hot room called the *caldarium*. Here, enslaved people would give massages to bath-goers using oil, and scrape off dirt from their bodies with a tool called a *strigil*. Afterwards, they would cool off in a cold pool called the *frigidarium*.

Religion

The Romans worshipped several gods and would offer sacrifices to them in return for their protection. Many felt that the empire had only been so successful because the gods were pleased with its citizens.

Religion in the Roman Empire revolved around three main gods: Jupiter, the god of the sky, Juno, the goddess of marriage, and Minerva, the goddess of wisdom. People believed that Jupiter protected the emperor, and after Augustus's rule began in 27 BCE, emperors themselves were also worshipped as gods. In parts of the Roman world, shrines, temples and statues were dedicated to emperors, and local people were expected to worship them. In return, emperors gifted communities with money. Festivals were also held where people would celebrate gods. The festival of *Saturnalia*, which honoured the god Saturn, involved singing and dancing, and saw roles in society reversed where enslaved people could be served by their enslavers.

Roman people grew worried when a new, unfamiliar religion called "Christianity" arrived in the empire in 50 CE. As Christianity spread throughout the empire, its followers were persecuted for their views. This changed in 312 CE when Emperor Constantine claimed that his victory at the Battle of Milvian Bridge had come from Jesus Christ. As a result, the emperor started treating Christians more fairly, and more people began to openly follow Christianity.

MINERVA   JUPITER   JUNO

The fall of the Roman Empire

As the Roman Empire grew to an extraordinary size, it became more difficult to control. There were economic problems, frequent civil wars and bitter battles for power. A single ruler could no longer look after the whole empire. In 330 CE, Emperor Constantine declared a new capital city of the empire – Constantinople, or Istanbul, Turkey, as we now know it. Eventually, in 395 CE, the empire was split into western and eastern sections, with Rome as the capital of the western half and Constantinople as the capital of the eastern half.

With the empire divided, Rome soon began to face a serious threat from a group of strong Germanic tribes called the "Visigoths". Following several violent attacks from these tribes, Roman troops were no longer able to defend themselves and their empire. What was once the strongest and mightiest army finally suffered defeat when the Visigoths conquered Rome in 476 CE and the emperor, Romulus Augustus, was forced to resign.

After over 1,000 years, the Roman Empire had finally come to an end. However, its influence would live on for centuries to come. The Romans had interacted with diverse groups of people and cultures, leaving their stamp across much of the world. From the roads we travel on to the languages we speak, we continue to see and experience the legacies of the ancient Romans all around us.

A Ladybird Book

collectable books for curious kids

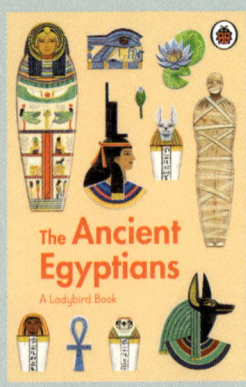

The Ancient Egyptians

9780241544174

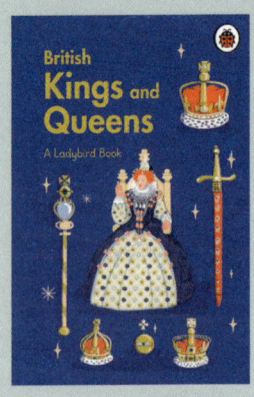

British Kings and Queens

9780241544167

The Romans

9780241544181

The Stone Age

9780241544198

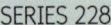

SERIES 228

Collect them all!

SERIES 208

- ☐ Animal Habitats
- ☐ Baby Animals
- ☐ Insects and Minibeasts
- ☐ Sea Creatures
- ☐ Trees

SERIES 218

- ☐ Electricity
- ☐ The Human Body
- ☐ The Solar System
- ☐ Trains
- ☐ Weather